Great Minds of Science

Sigmund Freud

Exploring the Mysteries of the Mind

John Bankston

 Enslow Publishers, Inc.

40 Industrial Road	PO Box 38
Box 398	Aldershot
Berkeley Heights, NJ 07922	Hants GU12 6BP
USA	UK

http://www.enslow.com

Library of Congress Cataloging-in-Publication Data

Bankston, John, 1974-
 Sigmund Freud: exploring the mysteries of the mind/
 John Bankston.— 1st ed.
  p. cm. — (Great minds of science)
 Includes bibliographical references and index.
 ISBN 0-7660-2336-2
 1. Freud, Sigmund, 1856-1939—Juvenile literature. 2. Psychoanalysts—
 Austria—Biography—Juvenile literature. I. Title. II. Series.
 BF109.F74B365 2006
 150.19'52'092—dc22
                                        2005013393

Printed in the United States of America

10 9 8 7 6 5 4 3 2 1

To Our Readers:
We have done our best to make sure all Internet Addresses in this book were
active and appropriate when we went to press. However, the author and the
publisher have no control over and assume no liability for the material
available on those Internet sites or on other Web sites they may link to. Any
comments or suggestions can be sent by e-mail to comments@enslow.com or
to the address on the back cover.

Illustration Credits: AP/ Wide World Photos, pp. 55, 59, 112; Enslow
Publishers, Inc., p. 17; Freud Museum, London, pp. 1, 8, 14, 19, 23,
26, 31, 39, 51, 53, 66, 71, 86, 103, 105, 106, 109; National Library of
Medicine, p. 97.

Cover Illustration: JupiterImages Corporation (background); Freud
Museum, London (inset).

Contents

Dreaming

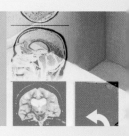

THE DOCTOR AWOKE WITH A START. Images from a nightmare still clung to him. It took a moment for him to realize that he was in Bellvue, a scenic resort near Vienna. He was vacationing there with his family. It was still very early. Usually, after such a dream, he would go back to sleep, or at least try to forget. That fateful July morning, he did neither.

Short and thin, a full beard concealed most of his face. His most distinctive feature was his eyes: dark and deep-set, they seemed to be always moving, always questioning. He had studied with some of the most respected doctors of his time at the University of Vienna. As a young adult, he had dreamed of becoming celebrated and successful. Instead, he was approaching forty with a struggling private practice and a growing family to support.

A Disturbing Scene

Even in daylight, the dream seemed disturbing. It began at a party. A young woman he had been treating burst into the room. She was in trouble. Leading her to a quiet corner, he angrily told her it was her own fault because she had ignored his advice. Fighting back tears the woman begged him to help—the choking in her chest and throat was terrible. She knew it would kill her.

In the dream, he asked her to open her mouth. She did so slowly and reluctantly, revealing a white patch and there, further down her throat, ugly gray scars. A small crowd of doctors gathered, wanting to help. One even injected the hapless patient with a solution of acid. "[Such] ingredients are not to be given so lightly. . . . Probably the syringe was not clean either," the doctor wrote in describing the dream.[1]

He knew it meant something. It just took him

a while to figure out what. The doctor believed right before a person falls asleep, the mind is sorting out the day's events. Dreams are a residue of that sorting process, representing "wish fulfillment." Scary or embarrassing dreams might not seem to fulfill a wish, but cracking the dream code could reveal what the patient truly wanted.

The Secret Revealed

The doctor's first serious attempt at discovering dreams' hidden meanings began that summer morning. He considered it so significant, he wondered if the Bellevue house would someday bear a marble plaque memorializing the event. "Here on July 24, 1895," it would read, *The Secret of the Dream* revealed itself to Dr. Sigmund Freud."[2]

The book he later wrote tried to unravel the mystery of dreams. It also helped make Dr. Sigmund Freud famous across the world.

The work he did was begun by others, thousands of years ago. Dreams have been seen as many things, from predictions for the future to messages from the gods. They have been described in religious texts.

Science and Philosophy

Freud was a man of science, but the concepts he explored were first described by philosophers. The Greek philosopher Aristotle's book *On Dreams*, written in 350 B.C. inspired some of Freud's work. Other ideas were first examined by Aristotle's teacher Plato, who lived in Athens from 427 B.C. to 347 B.C. Plato's *Republic* described three elements of the soul: the rational, the less rational and the impulsive irrational. Freud described three elements of the mind: the id, the ego, and the super ego.

Freud lived in a time when many people were examining the mind. Beginning in the eighteenth century, intellectuals, including scientists, writers, and

Sigmund Freud is pictured here circa 1891, just a few years prior to his breakthrough dream.

other artists, embraced a movement they called the "Enlightenment." Their goal was to "enlighten" their countrymen combating tyranny, superstition, and above all ignorance. It was a controversial movement that emphasized science over religion. "The key to the period seemed to be that the mind had become aware of itself," American writer, Ralph Waldo Emerson explained.[3]

Freud was also controversial. He began as a biologist, inspired by the scientists of his time. Yet he is best remembered for his work developing psychoanalysis. From its beginning, psychoanalysis was criticized as a pseudo science or false science. Many of its principles were subjective and difficult to prove. Scientists criticized Freud for making his results fit his theories instead of reaching a conclusion through experimentation, trial and error.

In his 1975 review "Victims of Psychiatry," Peter Medawar wrote, "The opinion is gaining ground that . . . psychoanalytic theory is the most stupendous intellectual [con] of the twentieth century . . . a vast structure of radically unsound design and with no posterity."[4]

Despite Medawar's criticism over twenty-five years ago, psychoanalysis not only survives, but Freud's work is enjoying a revival. Recently, sophisticated brain scans have supported some of his theories about the workings of the mind. In many ways, his quest for the solution to a still elusive riddle was ahead of its time. What determines who we are, what factors make up our personality, our choices, the very life we live? Is it just our parents, and how we are raised? Do the things that happen when we are infants determine the lives we will have as adults?

Understanding the Mind

Discovering how the body works is much easier. Dissecting a body reveals the anatomy—where the organs are located and the skeletal structure. Performing surgeries, and testing patients in labs demonstrate the way organs function—the beating of a heart, the working of the lungs, and so on.

The mind is more complex. Dissecting a brain does not reveal how emotions and personality are regulated. Even sophisticated medical devices leave many important questions unanswered.

Sigmund Freud did not treat mental illness with drugs. Instead he treated the depressed, the neurotic, the hysteric by just letting them talk, listening as he helped them to illuminate the dark shadows of their minds.

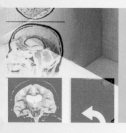

2

Turmoil

"WHEN I WAS A YOUNG MAN, I WENT FOR a walk on a Saturday in the town you were born in, wearing my best clothes and with a new fur cap on my head. Then a Christian comes along, knocks my cap into the mud with a single blow and shouts, 'Jew, get off the pavement!'"

The boy looked at his father. He was around twelve, and they paused during their walk for the story. The boy could not wait to find out what had happened. Was there an argument? Was there a fight? "What did you do?" he asked his father. "I stepped into the road and picked up my cap."[1]

That was it. Sigismund Freud was disappointed, but then he was used to being disappointed by his father. In the Freud family,

Jacob seemed weak and passive, in sharp contrast to his much younger wife, Amalia, who controlled the household.

Facing Prejudice

Sigismund Freud would grow up to be a man who rarely backed down from a fight. For Jewish people in the early 1800s, standing up for oneself was dangerous. In nineteenth-century Austria, anti-Semitism was rampant. Anti-Semitism is a hateful prejudice toward Jewish people. Strict laws determined how many Jews could live in certain areas and where they could go to school. There were restrictions on their religious ceremonies and on property owner-ship. Being born a Jew meant being born a second class citizen.

At this time, the Austro-Hungary Empire was a world power, like Italy, Spain, and France. The borders of these countries changed frequently as wars were won and lost, and explorers added colonies from distant lands. The Empire's success on the battlefield expanded the territory

Sigmund Freud and his father, Jacob, sit for a photograph in 1866.

they controlled beyond present day Austria and Hungary to include portions of what we know today as Poland, Czechoslovakia, and the Ukraine.

Although pleased with the addition of Galicia (part of present day Poland) the Empire was less excited about the addition of 200,000 Jews. In response, Jewish marriages and kosher food were heavily taxed as were ceremonial items required by the Jewish religion like special candles.

Freud's Father

It was into dirty, difficult Galicia that Jacob Freit was born. Like many Jews fearing discrimination, he later changed his name to "Freud," the German word for "joy." The name said it all. Jacob was an optimist; no matter how difficult the times were, he believed a better life was right around the corner. Earning a meager living selling scraps of clothing, his optimism seemed wildly unfounded.

By the time he was sixteen, he was in an

arranged marriage to Sally Kramer. While they were still teenagers, the couple would have two children, Emmanuel and Phillip. For much of their marriage Jacob was traveling with his grandfather, setting up a shop and keeping an apartment in distant Freiberg. Time with his family was rare.

By the late 1840s, Sally had died, and Jacob remarried. Little is known about his second wife, other than her name—Rebekka. She was listed as his wife on a permit to work in Freiberg. A few years later when he reapplied he was listed as a widower. This is the only evidence available that Jacob Freud was married twice before he met Amalia.

Freud's Mother

Amalia Nathanson was nineteen years old, from an upper middle class Jewish family. Twice her age, and with little money, Jacob Freud was hardly a "catch." In the 1800s, such age differences were common. Women often died in childbirth. Their husbands would go on to

A map showing the boundaries of Europe as they existed at the time of Freud's birth in 1856.

marry younger brides still capable of bearing children. Many men did not consider marriage until they were established professionally, so men in their thirties and forties often married teenagers.

Jacob was not just older. He was broke. He must have tried hard to be as charming as possible to get permission from Amalia's father. Whatever he did or said worked.

The newlyweds rented a large room over a blacksmith shop at Schlossergasse 117 in Freiberg, Moravia (now Czechoslovakia). Sigismund Schlomo Freud was born on May 6, 1856. His parent's nicknamed him "Sigi," and as their first born son he occupied a place of honor. His first memories included the spark and noise from the shop below. His other memories, however, were of sickness and of death.

Sibling Rivalry

Although money was tight, his parents would have a large family. While still in the small apartment, Amalia gave birth to a second son they named Julius. Sigi was enormously jealous of Julius. He had lost the attention from being an only child. He hated his younger brother. Over seventy years later, Freud would examine his rage, and remember that he was less than a year old at the time and still breastfeeding. "[It] is a remarkable fact that a child, even with an age difference of only eleven months, is not too young to take notice of what is happening. But what the child begrudges the unwanted intruder is not only suckling but all the other signs of maternal care."[2]

Less than a year later, Julius died from tuberculosis, and Sigi's jealousy turned to guilt. It lasted a lifetime.

Growing Up

Sigi grew up in a confusing, almost modern family. His older brothers were his mother's age, while his nephew (Emanuel's son) was actually older than he was. The entire family was in

A portrait of Freud as a child, painted by an unknown artist in 1868.

business together, buying wool cloth from locals, dying it a variety of colors and selling it to distant manufacturers.

Unlike Amalia's family, the Freud's were not observant Jews and rarely attended temple or celebrated religious holidays. As his mother endured life-threatening pregnancies, Sigi formed a close bond with his nursemaid. A Catholic, she often took Sigi to mass with her, which the Freuds did not seem to mind.[3] They were less understanding, however, when the nursemaid was caught stealing Amalia's jewelry. The Freuds then had her arrested.

Losing his nursemaid to jail, and his mother to difficult pregnancies, left young Sigi with a lot of time alone—time to wonder about the world. Jacob began teaching Sigi to read when he was just four. Soon, books became a means of escape for the boy. He especially enjoyed books on science and math.

Although life inside the Freud household was difficult, the situation for Austria's Jews began to improve by the 1850s. The Industrial Revolution had altered the way people worked. Machinery and factories slowly replaced farms as cities expanded. The new jobs needed people to do them and restrictions on Jewish migration were eased.

As significant as the Industrial Revolution was, other more violent revolutions swept across Europe. Inspired by revolts in the United States in 1776, and in France thirteen years later, by the middle eighteenth century many citizens across Europe were attempting to overthrow their leaders. Most failed.

Political Changes

In 1848, the leader of Austria, Emperor Ferdinand, brutally crushed a rebellion and executed its leaders. Despite his victory, he gave the throne to his teenage nephew, Franz Joseph. The new emperor realized if he did not offer greater freedom to his subjects, more revolutions were inevitable. He therefore enacted sweeping reforms, including laws liberating Jews. Once illegal religious ceremonies were now allowed and Jews were no longer restricted in their choice of profession. They could hold public office and own land. According to the new laws they were legally equal to the Christians.

In 1859, the Freud's moved to Leipzig in Germany. The next year they settled in the Leopoldstadt section of Vienna, Austria. By then Sigi had a new sibling, Anna, but his place of honor as the first born male remained.

Over seven thousand Jews lived in their new community. Although dirty and crowded, it was home to many successful Jewish professionals. The entire city's population was exploding. From the time of Freud's birth until 1880, the number of Jews grew from 10,000 to over 70,000—ten percent of Vienna's residents. It was the fastest growing major city in all of Europe. Bordered by the Danube River on one side and lush woods on the other three, it was world famous for music and architecture. It was also closer to Amalia's family—being able to rely on their financial help may have been part of why the family moved.

Education

During this time, Sigi Freud found he was under enormous pressure to be successful, to be a "good" son. No matter how hard he worked, no matter how well he did in school, he was never

A Freud family portrait circa 1879.

happy. While his mother was strict about his studies and grades, before long, it was Freud himself who became the harsh taskmaster. Even before he began going to school, he was reading works by William Shakespeare, and his father taught him Hebrew. A gift of a bible from Jacob to his son was inscribed, "It was in the seventh year of your age that the spirit of God began to move you to learning."[4]

In Austria, the demanding academic schools that educate elementary and high school students are called *gymnasiums*. By the time he was nine, Sigi Freud was ready to attend one. Although the brand new Sperl Gymnasium usually only admitted children older than ten, they made an exception for Sigi. By then he was already ahead of most kids his age. He excelled at reading and languages—studying Latin, Greek, English, Italian, French, and German. Freud was usually at the top of his class.

His family made many sacrifices to help him succeed. Sister Anna later recalled, "When I was eight years old, my mother, who was very musical, wanted me to study the piano and I began practicing by the hour. Though Sigismund's room was not near the piano, the sound disturbed him. He appealed my mother to remove the piano if she did not wish him to leave the house altogether. The piano disappeared, and with it, all opportunities for his sisters to become musicians."[5]

Sitting in a café with his parents, Sigi was twelve years old when a traveling poet approached their table. Jacob paid for a verse. It predicted a future for Sigi in the government. For a few years after the prediction, Freud considered becoming a lawyer. That changed one day after he heard doctor Carl Bruhl give a lecture (incorrectly attributed to Johann Wolfgang Goethe, the eighteenth century writer). As Freud later wrote in his autobiography, "theories of Darwin, which were then of topical interest, strongly attracted me, for they held out hopes of an extraordinary advance in our understanding of the world, and it was hearing Goethe's beautiful essay on nature read aloud at a popular lecture . . . just before I left school, that decided me to become a medical student."[6]

Charles Darwin's controversial book *The Origin of The Species* was published in 1859. An immediate success, its entire first printing sold out in a single day. In this and later works, Darwin set out his theories of evolution and survival of the fittest. The suggestion that man was biologically connected to all animals and that they evolved over time rather than created whole by God was attacked by many religious leaders. Although in the twenty-first century, evolution is accepted as fact by most scientists, it remains a controversial subject. Many nonscientists view evolution as still just a theory and

Freud's sister Anna is pictured here in a photograph taken in 1880.

legal battles over its teaching in schools have gone on for nearly a century.

To the teenage Freud, it was the opening shot of a brave new battle in the war to separate science from religion, and develop theories based only on rigorous research. By the time he graduated the gymnasium in 1873, Freud was a young man prepared to take on as much controversy as Darwin.

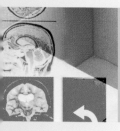

3

Choices

FORTY YEARS AGO THEY WERE A FAMILIAR sight alongside nearly every street, from cities to small towns. Today they have gone the way of phone booths and television antennas. Revolving just outside a business selling haircuts, barber's poles featured stripes in alternating colors, usually red and white. Few customers understood the colors' significance.

In the 1500s, barbers were elevated to the level of surgeons, allowing them to do more than just cut hair. They also cut people. The red stripe was for blood, the white for bandages. Bleeding—cutting a sick person to "release" disease—was a preferred method of treatment. Barbers often had limited medical training;

their education was based more on superstition than science.

As a treatment for illness, bleeding was often worse than the disease. Indeed, George Washington is widely believed to have died partially as the result of overzealous bleeding, when he was drained of over five pints of blood during his last days.[1] From the time of Freud's youth it would take nearly a century before medical treatments began to resemble techniques we would recognize today.

Advances in medicine generally flow from a hypothesis—an idea presented by a doctor. The theory is carefully tested in a laboratory, usually by experimentation on numerous subjects, from tiny mice to human beings. Eventually, successful surgical techniques, medicine, or other ideas were implemented. This is the area of medicine that attracted young Sigismund Freud. He was not interested in performing surgery or making rounds. He was interested in research, becoming a medical scientist and learning as much as he possibly could about how the body functions.

College

Freud enrolled at the University of Vienna. The school attracted some of the best educators in Europe and students from as far away as the United States. Transformed by its increasingly well-educated populace, the city was developing a reputation for research equal to the one it already had for coffee shops and music.

During his first year at the University, Freud encountered some anti-Semitism, but he wrote, "I never understood why I should be ashamed of my descent, or as everyone was beginning to say, my race."[2] Making things easier was the fact that the student body was around forty percent Jewish, along with nearly a third of the teachers in the medical program. Still, despite all this, just as his father had done, Sigismund Freud would adopt a less Jewish name: Sigmund.

Freud probably would have been happy remaining a student his whole life. He loved the

Freud is pictured here at age eighteen, standing next to his mother.

seemingly endless amounts of studying, the careful experimentation and lectures given by some of the most respected doctors in Europe. His time at the University was so fulfilling he stayed there for nearly a decade, years longer than other medical students.

This was a luxury his family could not afford. They tried to help him as best they could, but Jacob Freud never earned much of a living. Into his sixties, Jacob relied on his sons, Emmanuel and Phillip for help. Sigmund Freud would also rely on others, taking loans from friends and teachers until he was well into his thirties.

In his first year at the University, Freud's life would have looked familiar to many twenty-first-century freshmen. He filled his free time with all-night discussions about the meaning of life, the sciences, and the future. Young women were also discussed, but Freud was painfully shy and inexperienced with dating. His closest relationship had been an unrequited crush on a girl named Gisella. He was sixteen at the time, she was not yet twelve, and probably unaware of his interest. Despite that, he wrote about her for years.

Father Figure

While he was growing up, Freud was disappointed by what he saw as his father's weakness. So as an adult, he sought out strong father figures for guidance—men like Ernst Brücke. Brücke, the head of the University's Psychological Institute, was a leader in the revolutionary Helmholtz School of Medicine. Its members believed principles of physics could be applied to living things. Physics, the study of energy and matter and how the two interact would have a tremendous influence on the twentieth century. Responsible for everything from the atomic bomb to space travel, in the nineteenth century its principles were beginning to be applied to medical science.

Despite being three times Freud's age, Brücke was far from set in his ways. Indeed, he embraced new scientific movements and sought ways to apply them to medicine. Freud's biographer, Ernest Jones, recalled Brücke as the owner of "terrifying, blue eyes," rather shy, but stern.[3] Despite his forbidding manner he was open to student opinion. "To the student who proved his ability," Jones later explained, "he was a most benevolent father, extending counsel and protection far beyond scientific matters. He respected the student's own ideas, encouraged original work and sponsored talents even if they deviated considerably from his own opinions."[4]

In the classroom Brücke maintained almost military discipline. Cutting class was unacceptable. After Freud was tardy once, he never did it again. He did not want to have to face those "terrifying, blue eyes."

Brücke, like Freud, valued learning and knowledge for its own sake. The two men would later be remembered as iconoclasts—people who break away from the accepted ways of doing things. Still, even in the 1880s Freud remained comfortable performing menial tasks just as medical students had for decades.

Discovering by Research

In his third year at the university, Freud's zoology professor sponsored him on a trip to the Zoological Experimentation Station in Trieste. For weeks, Freud sliced open four hundred eels in an effort to find just one with male sex organs. Coming up empty, he theorized that eels do not develop male organs until later in their life span. He was later proven correct.

Returning to school, Freud focused on laboratory research. Once he discovered that gold chloride was perfect for staining nerve cell samples so they could be viewed under a microscope. He also did work on the nerve cells of lampreys, which were remarkably similar to the spinal cells in more advanced organisms— possible evidence of evolution.

By then Freud realized even the most tedious job could lead to unexpected conclusions. While working in Brücke's laboratory, Freud met another father figure—Josef Breuer, a respected doctor and research scientist. He took a liking to the young Freud, and by 1881 was giving Freud money every month—a loan Sigmund never had to repay. Years later, Freud would write a letter admitting, "I came to know the helplessness of poverty and continually feared it."[5]

Medical research almost guaranteed poverty. It was the career choice for children of the rich whose families could support their low paying ambitions. Freud did not fall into this category, but he still was not interested in any other type of work.

Then, in a single moment, everything changed.

Meeting His Wife

In his early twenties, Freud could be very self-centered. He did not worry about his family's financial difficulties and he rarely paid attention to anyone beyond his professors and close circle of friends. He was not the only one.

As his sister Anna later recalled: "One would have imagined that the presence in the house of five young women would have held some attraction for these young men, but they seemed less interested in entertainment than in scientific discussion with our learned brother and disappeared into his room with scarcely a glance at us!"[6]

Then, one day he arrived home to the usual crowd of his sister's girlfriends. This time he did not push past them on the way to his room. Instead, he paused. One of them caught his eye.

She was eating an apple. Sigmund Freud went back to where she was sitting, and began to talk to her. Something evidently drew him to her, something that set her apart from everyone else. Even Freud was not sure what it was, but pointed out, "When making a decision of minor importance, I have always found it advantageous to consider all the pros and cons. In vital matters, however, such as the choice of a mate or a profession, the decision should come from the unconscious, from somewhere within ourselves."[7]

It was love at first sight. Twenty-six year old Freud began spending a lifetime's worth of pent up energy on a single person. He wrote her poetic love letters, while complaining about his awkwardness, confessing, "I think there is a general enmity [hostility] between artists and those engaged in the details of scientific work. We know that they possess in their art the master key to open with ease all female hearts, whereas we stand helpless at the strange design of the lock."[8]

Freud did all he could to "unlock" Martha's heart. He dated her regularly with a chaperone. He kissed her chastely during long goodbyes. He confessed his every thought and emotion, often as soon as he became aware of them. His greatest addiction was cigars—at his peak he would smoke twenty a day. He once told Martha, "Smoking is indispensable if one has nothing to kiss."[9]

Less than two months after they met, he asked her to marry him. She said, "Yes."

It would be a long and secretive engagement. Freud was penniless, with few prospects, while Martha, like Freud's mother, grew up in a secure, middle class home. Her grandfather was a rabbi, her father was a merchant who later worked for a well-known economist. His death when she was eighteen left the family facing an uncertain financial future. Her mother assumed that when Martha married, she would marry well.

Freud knew this. He realized the only way he could marry Martha Bernays was if he lived up to her family's expectations. At that moment, his career path changed.

Career Opportunities

Jacob Freud always encouraged his son to follow his heart, taking whatever career path interested him most. Brücke had a different opinion. He "strongly advised me, in view of my bad financial position, to abandon my theoretical career. I followed his advice, left the physiological laboratory and entered the General Hospital."[10]

Freud's future wife, Martha Bernays, in a photograph taken in 1880.

39

In 1882, Freud started at the bottom, working as a clinical assistant or Aspirant at the General Hospital. Just like medical students working as residents today, Freud endured very long hours, very little pay, and even less sleep. Residents "rotate" through the different specialties within a hospital: Freud spent time working with the surgeons, the neurologists, and the psychiatrists. His exposure to a physician's life did not make it any more attractive to him.

By May of 1883, he'd risen to the position of Sekundararzt in the psychiatry department, a year later he was made Senior Sekundararzt, which made him something of a chief resident in the department. Despite his progress, Freud had little taste for the work.

His boss, Theodor Meynert, did not like psychiatry either. A heavy drinker, he had little patience for his patients. To him they were just research specimens. His psychiatric clinic doubled as a laboratory, but the work he did just made him more certain that they were incurable. Despite his prejudices, some of his theories were proven a century later: "The more that psychiatry seeks and finds its scientific basis in a deeply and finely grained understanding of the structure [of the brain], the more it elevates itself to the status of a science that deals with causes."[11]

Epileptics and many others institutionalized during Freud's time actually had treatable neurological conditions. Ironically, he moved from psychiatry toward neurology because he believed the former profession wasted time on the untreatable. Freud had a much clearer idea of what he did not want to do than what he did.

When he was not working or corresponding with Martha, he was writing medical journal articles—the best known from that period he titled, "On Coca." He finished it in a hurry after his fiancée unexpectedly invited him for a visit. He had not seen her in over a year and needed to complete the article before leaving.

Sigmund Freud wanted to be well known. Unfocused and uncertain about his career, he knew researching and writing about a miracle drug could change his life. Doctors and scientists who make such discoveries often become very successful, whether from unveiling a brand new drug or simply finding a different use for an existing one. As he finished the paper, Freud was convinced he had found the miracle drug others missed.

"I take very small doses of it regularly against depression and against indigestion, and with the most brilliant success," he later wrote Martha Bernays.[12]

Unfortunately Freud's drug was not a dream cure. By the twentieth century it would have a well-earned reputation as a dangerous drug. But in the nineteenth century, it would be added to everything from cough medicine to soda pop. Freud's miracle drug was cocaine.

Freud began taking the drug himself. Nervous in crowds, and uncomfortable around unfamiliar people, Freud loved the sudden boost of confidence cocaine provided. He even mailed a small sample to his fiancée, "to make her strong and give her cheeks a red color."[13]

By 1891, Freud had stopped recommending the drug.

Although his writing did not make Freud rich and famous, it helped earn him the position of lecturer in Neuropathology at the University of Vienna. The job was very low paying (about $2,000 annually in today's money) but highly respected. It was considered a step toward becoming a successful doctor. With the appointment six months away, Freud applied for a grant to increase his knowledge.

The grant was approved, and in 1885 he left for Paris, France, to study with the neuropathologist, Jean Martin Charcot.

Life in Paris

The journey away from Vienna put Sigmund Freud closer to his ambitions. Charcot was a celebrity. He lived like a prince, and had the looks and presence of a stage actor. Fabulously wealthy, Charcot lived in a huge château surrounded by lush landscaping. He threw fabulous parties where he offered his guests demonstrations of the hypnotic technique that made him famous.

By then he had taken what many thought was a magic trick and turned it into a diagnostic tool for treating a growing problem. Named for Hypnos, the Greek god of sleep, hypnosis is a world somewhere between sleeping and waking, a mental state that is neither completely unconscious nor conscious. Four thousand years ago it was described by Egyptian hieroglyphics. It grew popular in eighteenth-century Europe after a Vienna doctor named Franz Anton Mesmer applied magnets to patients in an attempt to cure them by altering their mental state. Although the word "mesmerized" came from his efforts, it would be doctor James Braid, who in 1843 referred to the trancelike state as "hypnosis."

Charcot was quite arrogant as a practitioner—walking into a room, he would tell a patient what their ailment was before they even said a word. Still, the doctor had a profound influence on Freud. His work of examining how the mind is connected to illness and his hypnosis sessions did not provide immediate cures, but his efforts inspired other doctors. Doctors like Sigmund Freud.

Studying Hysteria

By the late 1800s, many women were diagnosed with a condition commonly called "hysteria." Consisting of physical symptoms like paralysis that did not have an apparent cause, most doctors believed it was related to a malfunctioning uterus (hysteria is from the Greek word for womb) and dismissed it as a "woman's disease." Many of its sufferers were believed to be pretending so they could get the attention of others.

Charcot was one of the first doctors to look at the mental causes for hysteria. He did more than study the women. He took their complaints seriously. Using hypnosis, he demonstrated how hysteria was the result of a very real psychological problem. He found that it was not from a physical disease, nor were the victims faking.

After putting the patient in a deep, trance like state, Charcot would give what is called a "post-hypnotic suggestion." For example, he might tell a patient that when she woke up, she would be able to move her paralyzed arm. Then he would take the patient out of the trance. Sure enough, the patient was able to move her limb. Once awake, she could not have moved the arm if the injury was real. If she was faking, it would have been revealed during hypnosis.

Foundation for Later Work

Witnessing the older doctor's work, Freud imagined how he would interact with his own future patients. Before Freud left Paris, Charcot discussed the subject that would later dominate Freud's work: sexuality. "[In] such cases it is always a question of [sexuality]—always, always, always."[14]

Charcot did not make this comment from a lectern or in the pages of a scientific journal. He said it as an offhand comment at a party, surrounded by admirers. Freud was nearby, wondering why the eminent doctor would keep such an astonishing idea so quiet. Freud soon found out.

In 1886, Freud's Paris sojourn ended and he returned to Vienna, a city he would often claim to loathe, but a city which claimed him until he was well past eighty years of age.

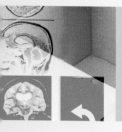

4

Chimney Sweeping

BARELY SETTLED IN VIENNA, SIGMUND Freud was already creating controversy. In the fall of 1886, Sigmund Freud presented what he considered a groundbreaking paper: "Male Hysteria." Speaking to the members of the Viennese Society of Physicians, he wanted to demonstrate what Charcot taught him. Since it was proven that hysteria was not linked to the uterus, why couldn't men also suffer from it?

When he was done, an older surgeon angrily objected. The very name "hysteria," was connected to the womb. How could Freud entertain such a notion? Years later, he would still bitterly recall that "I met with a bad reception. Persons of authority, such as the chairman . . . declared that what I said was incredible. The impression that the high authorities had rejected my innovations remained unshaken."[1]

Freud actually exaggerated the mood of the crowd—a number of the doctors *were* receptive to his theories. Besides, others had discussed male hysteria before Freud did. Still, there is no question that he was far from the favored son returning home. In 1886, Sigmund Freud was as unestablished as his theories.

In the spring, he had quit his job at the General Hospital and "set out a shingle," renting an office displaying a sign advertising his medical practice. On Easter Sunday, readers of local medical journals and newspapers might have seen his small notice: " Herr Dr. Sigmund Freud, Docent in Nervous Diseases at the University of Vienna, has returned from his study trip to Berlin and six months in Paris and now resides at Rathausstrasse No. 7, from 1 to 2:20 P.M."[2]

New patients were hardly beating down his door. The few he had were referrals from other doctors, especially Josef Breuer. With quite a bit of spare time, he did research at Meynert's laboratory, translated Charcot's books into German and worked at the university. He continued to rely on friends, and anyone who had more money than he did. In those early days, that was just about all of them. Still, that year he believed his career was going well enough to finally get married.

Married Life

Sigmund Freud and Martha Bernays's four-year engagement concluded in 1886. Freud demanded a small civil ceremony, which took place on September 13. However, the Austrian government recognized only religious services. In order to make it legal, the couple were married again in a Jewish ceremony two days later.

They settled into a four-room apartment on the Maria Theresienstrasse. Their building, called the House of Atonement, rested on ashes from the tragic Ring Theatre fire, where many had died. Most potential tenants were too superstitious to live there, but Freud was not worried about ghosts, only saving money. With such a grim history, the apartment was a bargain.

In his letters, Freud had been an ardent and passionate romantic. But as a husband, he was distant and demanding. Martha was docile even by Victorian standards. Freud banned any religious observances in the household, and she

Sigmund and Martha Freud's wedding portrait.

later told her cousin that "not being able to light the Sabbath lights on the first Friday night after her marriage was one of the more upsetting experiences of her life."[3]

Martha rarely questioned her husband and he did not seek out her opinions. Later, he would discuss new theories with her sister, Minna Bernays, an unmarried woman who moved in to help with their growing family.

Freud's Children

Since Martha's father died a few years before she was engaged, it was traditional for them to name their first born son after him. But Freud was not interested in tradition. When they had a son in 1889, Freud named him Jean Martin, after Charcot. Two years earlier, he named their first child Mathilde, after Breuer's wife.

In 1890, their son Oliver was named after Oliver Cromwell (the famous British General who became head of the British government after the overthrow of the monarchy in 1649). In 1892, Ernst was named after Brücke; and the following

Sigmund and Martha Freud with their youngest daughter Anna in 1899.

year, Sophie was named after the wife of Joseph Pantheth, one of his financial supporters. In 1895, the couple's last child was named Anna— not after Freud's sister, but after a favored patient, Anna Hammerschlag Lichtheim.

With a growing family, the couple outgrew their apartment. Although the two began looking for a new place together, Freud discovered an apartment on his own one day that he loved. He rented it before showing it to Martha.

Located at 19 Berggasse, it was in a seedy neighborhood, the building itself dark and cramped. Martha was disappointed when she saw it, but she realized that her husband had his heart set on the space. A friend of his had lived in the building during college; he even had the office organized in his mind. When he received his first couch in 1890, everything seemed perfect. One of the most famous pieces of furniture in history, the couch was where patients would comfortably recline, while Freud sat at their head, out of sight and listening intently.

The new home would be the last one they would have in Vienna.

"Anna O"

As his family grew, so did Freud's opportunities. Two minds are often better than one, especially in

The couch once used by Freud's patients, draped with a Persian rug, as it appears today at the Sigmund Freud Museum in London.

scientific research. In the late 1880s, Freud began working with Josef Breuer. Back in 1880, when Freud was still a student, Breuer had begun treating a friend of Martha's. Bertha Pappenheim (immortalized as "Anna O"), arrived at Breuer's office enduring headaches, partial paralysis of the limbs and even hallucinations. He described the unmarried twenty-one-year-old as, "Intelligence considerable; excellent memory, astonishingly acute [gift for] combinations and keen intuition, hence attempts to deceive her always fail."[4]

Anna O grew up in a very conservative Jewish household, with few options outside of a traditional marriage. She retreated into her own imagination. The world disappeared as she was entertained by what the patient called her own "private theatre."

During her time with Breuer she began seeing skeletons and snakes. For days Anna could not speak in her native German, communicating only in English or in French. Battling her condition, she took the first steps in the treatment Freud later perfected.

Working with Breuer, she realized her condition improved after she discussed what was troubling her. Once, she found herself unable to drink a simple glass of water. Parched and scared, she told Breuer about witnessing a dog sipping from a friend's water glass. The act disgusted her, but as soon as she described it, her swallowing problem disappeared. Anna O called it "the talking cure," or "chimney sweeping."

When Freud returned to Vienna from his time in Paris, Breuer had greeted the doctor with a hug and a promise to help. Yet as important as Breuer's patient referrals and loans were, they were insignificant compared to the promise of the "talking cure."

The Development of Psychoanalysis

The treatment of hysterics was haphazard, even cruel. Some patients were given powerful drugs including morphine and chloroform. Others were put on very restrictive diets or plunged into ice cold water. For all his advances, even Charcot experimented with hanging them from an iron harness attached to the ceiling of his office. Freud treated hysterics at first with hypnosis, but later used electrical stimulation.

Heinrich Erb was a German neurologist who pioneered the technique of connecting wires to patients and sending weak jolts of electricity through their body. An hysteric's "paralyzed limbs" would move and tingle. American doctor Weir Mitchell combined electricity with massage, diet, and rest cures.

Freud used both techniques. After a patient took the rest cure, leaving for a spa, the patient rarely returned to his office. This was not the best way to maintain an income. More importantly, the treatment seemed ineffective. Their symptoms only disappeared at first, but he realized that was probably because a doctor was finally listening to them. In a lecture, Freud explained "I soon came to dislike hypnosis for it was a temperamental, and one might almost say, a mystical ally. When I found that, in spite of all my efforts, I could not succeed in bringing more than a fraction of my patients into a hypnotic state, I determined to give up hypnosis and to make the cathartic procedure ("the talking cure") independent of it."[5]

Still, hypnosis had one benefit Freud continued to explore. Hypnotized patients usually grew closer to him, more trusting. It was a

Freud's desk on display at the Sigmund Freud Museum in London. Freud died while living in London in 1939. His daughter, Anna, would continue to live in this same home until her death in 1982. The home was then restored and opened as the Freud Museum in 1986.

process Freud later wrote about as "transference." In transference, earlier experiences that are brought up in therapy result in the patient behaving toward their doctor as if he were a significant person in the event. Although negative transference can slow down the process (if the therapist reminds them of a hated uncle, for example), positive transference could be helpful. Long after he abandoned hypnosis, transference became a vital part of the therapy.

The therapy evolved into what Freud called "psychoanalysis." The doctor did not take all the credit, as he pointed out during a lecture at Massachusetts's Clark University: "If it is a merit to have brought psychoanalysis into being, that merit is not mine. I had no share in its earliest beginnings. I was a student and working for my final examinations at the time when another Viennese physician, Dr. Josef Breuer, first in 1880–1882, made use of this procedure on a girl who was suffering from hysteria [Anna O]."[6]

If "Anna O" and Breuer had taken the first few strides of psychoanalysis, Freud was now ready to run a marathon.

The Science of Analysis

He had the beginnings for a scientific experiment, complete with controls and variables. The control group contained the other women, women with similar symptoms who were treated with electroshock. The variable group contained the women he treated with the talking cure. If the variable group improved more than the control, then Freud would gain confidence in his new approach. Although Freud continued to work with Breuer, writing case studies that would become the book *Studies on Hysteria*, the younger doctor's interest was already focusing on the "talking cure."

Beginning in 1889, and continuing for several years, his talking cure focused on several women whose almost daily treatment gave Freud a steady income. The question was whether the time and money his patients invested was worthwhile.

"Frau Emmy N" (whose real name was Baroness Fanny Moser) was a forty-year-old widow whose symptoms were similar to "Anna O's." The unlucky thirteenth of fourteen children, her life was a series of tragic events. For fun, her siblings threw dead animals at her when she was five. Two years later she witnessed her sister lying in a casket. At fifteen her mother suffered a stroke and it was Frau Emmy who found her on the floor.

Four years after that, when her mother died, it was Frau Emmy who came home to find the body. Years later, her much older husband died unexpectedly in the bedroom where Frau Emmy was recovering from a second pregnancy.

These traumas influenced her life, leaving her broken and vulnerable. When she arrived at the doctor's office, she did more than just tell her story. She greatly influenced his therapeutic method by insisting that Freud stop "asking 'where this or that came from' but let her tell me what she had to say."[7]

Her treatment was brief. He pronounced her cured after less than two months. Unfortunately, she would battle mental illness off and on for years. In the beginning, he did not realize patients fighting mental illness can relapse. Just like the physically sick, their symptoms often return after a short time away from therapy.

Although Freud recognized how witnessing so much death traumatized Frau Emmy, he believed the primary reason for her illnesses was "living for years in a state of sexual abstinence."[8]

"Katharina"

Freud's work with "Frau Emmy N" was nothing compared to the "magic" he worked in a single session with "Katharina." Traumatized by her father's attempted rape, followed by witnessing him sexually abusing her sister, Katharina met with Freud while he was on vacation. The doctor's reputation was growing, and she hoped he could cure her anxiety, chest pains, and shortness of breath accompanied by enormous guilt. The guilt she felt was a result of her parents's divorce after she told her mother about the incidents with her father.

Freud got her to "open up," talking about the complicated feelings she had toward her father, mother, and sister. He quickly connected the woman's symptoms to the abuse. In an attempt to either conceal her identity or minimize the trauma, he altered her relationships when he wrote about the case, making the father an uncle, the sister a cousin.

Results

After a few years and a few patients, Freud was noticing what Breuer noticed with Anna O a decade before. By retrieving a memory buried in the unconscious, a patient's physical problems often either improved or disappeared entirely.

Freud's system of psychoanalysis (as he would name it in 1896) was an intensive program with one hour sessions every day, six days a week (on Sunday, his patients rested). The therapeutic technique would make him famous.

By the early 1890s, Freud believed he and Breuer had accumulated enough research to write about their work and publish the results. The older man was not convinced, however. After all, the "talking cure" had barely been tested. Worse, a number of the patients were not "cured." It appeared to be more effective than electroshock, but with only a dozen subjects, Breuer believed there were too few for a decent study.

Freud overcame his partner's objections. In 1893, they co-authored an article entitled "Preliminary Communications: On the Physical

Mechanism of Hysterical Phenomena." Two years later they published *Studies on Hysteria*. Despite the small number of subjects, the men described a range of symptoms for the psychological disease of emotional hysterical breakdown.

Some doctors were impressed with their work, but many others complained that it suffered from two primary flaws. First, Breuer and Freud used too few subjects for a conclusion. The second complaint followed Freud for the rest of his career and even endures today. This complaint was that Freud believed every symptom, every problem, could be linked directly to some sexual issue.

Freud and Sex

Several of the women Freud treated *were* suffering from the aftermath of sexual trauma. However, several others were recovering from the deaths of close family members. Rather than identifying that as the cause for their hysterical symptoms, Freud felt sex was again, the culprit. If they did not discuss it in therapy, Freud thought they were repressing (holding back),

Freud's sons, Ernst, Martin, and Oliver, circa 1900.

thereby making it even more significant than if they had actually talked about it.

Freud would clarify these beliefs in his 1898 paper, "Sexuality in the Aetiology of the Neurosis." "Exhaustive research during the last few years," he wrote, "have led me to recognize that the most immediate and for practical purposes, the most significant cases of neurotic illnesses are to be found in factors arising from sexual life."[9]

Freud's focus on sex as the core reason for his patient's complaints created a permanent rift with his collaborator. Breuer saw hysterical illness as a more complex disease, created by a variety of factors. "I confess that the plunging into sexuality in theory and practice is not to my taste," Breuer later told a colleague.[10]

The older doctor went further, admitting he "suppressed a large number of quite interesting details" because his partner wanted the conclusion to be consistent. Breuer removed any suggestions from his writing that something other than sexual trauma could lead to hysterical illness.[11]

Freud felt like an explorer in a brave new world, slashing through the landscape of contradictory opinion, knowing he was right and having little tolerance for shades of gray. "One cannot do without people who have the courage to think new things before they can demonstrate them," he later pointed out.[12]

A Falling Out

Despite the loans, the referrals, indeed even Breuer's responsibility for helping Freud develop what he would call psychoanalysis, by the time their book was published, the younger doctor was distancing himself. Earlier, Freud complained Breuer was holding him back. By 1896, he had stopped speaking to Breuer. Many years later Freud would pass the doctor on the street and pointedly ignore him.

It was a pattern Freud would repeat for the rest of his life. He would form a bond with a man he respected, working hard on a mutual project, and then later completely freeze him out over a disagreement.

5

The Dream

IT WAS 1888 AND WILHELM FLIESS WAS impressed. The Berlin doctor mainly treated nose and throat problems, but it was a lecture about the mind that inspired him. After the speech was over, he came up and congratulated the speaker. Sigmund Freud was grateful for the compliments.

"Esteemed friend and colleague," Freud wrote Fliess a short time later, "my letter of today is occasioned by business, but I must introduce it by confessing that I entertain hopes of continuing the relationship with you."[1]

Throughout Freud's life, when one friendship cooled another took its place. Although many of his hundreds of letters to Fliess seem more personal than professional, considering the work Fliess was doing, it is understandable.

Josef Breuer was a father figure, but Fliess was practically a twin brother. Photographs of him and Freud reveal two men with nearly identical bushy beards, long moustaches, high foreheads and even similar earlobes. While Breuer was uncomfortable with Freud's sexual focus, Fliess encouraged it.

Fliess believed that men and women share sexual and emotional qualities with each other. Today the theory hardly seems radical. However many of his other ideas were as mystical and superstitious as anything described centuries earlier. For example, he believed everything from heart trouble to difficult pregnancies began in the nose.

Besides the nose, Fliess focused on numbers. A woman's menstrual cycle is twenty-eight days. He believed men have a similar cycle, which he decided was twenty-three days. He relied on those two numbers to resolve many different problems. Despite his outlandish ideas, Fliess's support of Freud during a difficult time helped Freud develop the rough ideas for many of his psychoanalytic principles.

Physics and Chemistry

Looking at the personality as an energy system, Freud applied the laws of physics he had learned under Brücke. He focused especially on the Law of Conservation of Energy: energy cannot be created or destroyed, it can only be changed.

Shortly after completing his work with Breuer in the early spring of 1895, Freud began working feverishly on what he would call the "Psychology for Neurologists." Freud applied rigid rules to the seemingly random behavior of hysterics, relying on specific principles and language familiar to the era's chemists.

His focus was so fine he could not concentrate on anything else. At home he

This photograph of Freud was taken in 1906.

was brooding and distant. Even sessions with patients seemed like distractions.

In a few months, Freud completed a rough draft for theories that would become his life's work. He would spend decades examining "drives"—what motivates people to behave as they do, "repression and defense"—ways the unconscious mind hides information from the conscious and the barriers patients put up to avoid dealing with it. He looked at "mental economy" which he saw as the battling forces of various energies. He explored how a person is a "wishing animal."[2]

After nearly six months, the doctor was ready for a second opinion. On October 8, he sent a draft to his friend Fliess. As soon as it left Freud's hands, he began to feel terrible. He sank into a deep depression, filled with self doubt and hatred for what he had written. He even began questioning "the mental state in which I hatched the *Psychology*."[3]

Later called *The Project for a Scientific Psychology*, it would become Freud's unfinished symphony. He would refer to it often, borrowing from some sections, refining others, even dismissing portions as he championed new theories. Although he never completed it, the work was called Newtonian. This is because it applied the laws of motion (developed by Sir Isaac Newton) to the way the mind expends energy through various emotional states.

By 1895, Freud had a published book and the beginnings of what he thought would be an earth-shattering theory of psychology. Yet neither event was as important as what took place in a single night while he was asleep.

An Enlightening Dream

It was early summer, and Freud was enjoying his annual vacation. Resting with his family at the Vienna resort of Bellevue, he had the dream that changed his life. Inside a large hall, he dreamed Martha and he were greeting guests. Suddenly "Irma" arrived.

Irma was based in part on Emma Eckstein, a patient shared by Fliess and Freud. Eckstein nearly died after Fliess performed an operation. Eventually, Fliess realized something had gone wrong and scheduled a second operation. Freud witnessed that surgery along with the bloody aftermath when Fliess extracted infected gauze from her nose. He'd accidentally left it there after the first operation. It nearly cost the woman her life. Freud refused to blame Fliess. He believed her physical symptoms and lengthy postoperative recovery came from her hysteria.

In his dream, while Freud examined Irma, a small crowd of doctors gathered. After the dream, Freud could identify them: Fliess, Breuer, and his children's doctor, Oscar Rie. They all wanted to help. Freud believed Rie and Breuer were the ones responsible for Irma's distress. Rie in fact made it worse.

When he woke up, Freud began to think about the dream. He knew that it meant something. It just took him a while to figure out what. The Irma dream was Freud's first serious attempt at discovering a dream's hidden meanings.

The dream referenced a time when, as a

young doctor, one of Freud's patients died. The crowding, unhelpful group of doctors represented doctors who had been unhelpful to him with his practice, the doctors who tried to hold back the progress of psychoanalysis— especially Breuer. Fliess represented the doctors who were on his side, "good" doctors who would help his patients, and also the cause of psychoanalysis.[4]

Freud's detailed explanation of the dream's meaning still left out a number of important facts. Dreams were riddles. Freud wanted to write a book solving them. Such a project could earn him respect among fellow doctors who had dismissed psychoanalysis. He also believed a book on dreams might interest the average reader, so he tried to make it accessible.

Freud hoped his book on dreams would fulfill his own dreams for wealth and fame.

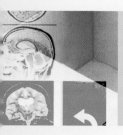

6

Complexes

AT TWELVE YEARS OLD, A POET PREDICTED greatness for Sigmund Freud. In Greek mythology, a far worse prediction was given to Laius, the ruler of Thebes. It was predicted that someday his newborn son would murder him.

Hoping to change the future, Laius ordered a slave to take his son and kill him. Pitying the child, the slave instead gave the baby boy to a shepherd. Laius's son would be named Oedipus. He grew up never knowing that the shepherd's family was not really his own. Years later, while traveling as an adult, Oedipus encountered a hostile man blocking a road. The two argued and Oedipus killed him.

Later, after saving the city of Thebes from a deadly monster, Oedipus was made the city's ruler and allowed to marry the dead king's wife, Jocasta. The couple would have four children. Many years afterward, Oedipus discovered that the man he killed on the road that day was his real father, and that Jocasta, his wife, was his mother. After learning this, the couple decided to punish themselves for their sin. Jocasta took her own life while Oedipus blinded himself by driving pins into his eyes.

As a teenager, Freud had read Sophocles's dramatic re-telling of the myth of Oedipus, *Oedipus Rex*. Decades later, he imagined a very similar drama going on in every young child's life, but with less tragic conclusions.

"Seduction Theory"

On April 21, 1896, Sigmund Freud had presented his "seduction theory" to the Society for Psychiatry and Neurology. Entitled, "The Etiology of Hysteria," it relied on data from eighteen patients and offered to the public a theory he had been privately discussing with Fliess for some time. Along with hysterics, he included a group he called "obsessional neurotics"—patients who displayed similar behaviors to hysterics but without any physical symptoms. He believed the patients he had treated were all suffering the effects of childhood sexual abuse.

This was scandalous. While commonly discussed today, in Freud's time such topics were rarely dealt with—even by physicians. The head of the Society for Psychiatry and Neurology, Richard von Krafft-Ebing, listened to Freud's presentation and said afterwards, "It sounds like a scientific fairy tale."[1]

The same year he presented the theory, Freud's father died. Jacob Freud's death occurred when his son was engaged in heavy self-analysis and self-doubt. Just a year after publicly presenting his theory, Freud abandoned it. "Such widespread perversion against children is scarcely probable," he wrote to Fliess.[2]

The Oedipus Complex

Without the seduction theory, Freud needed a better explanation for the source of neuroses.

He discovered it in his self-analysis, and his memory of the book *Oedipus Rex*. Freud believed that an unfulfilled wish of boys, at around age four or five, was to marry their mothers. They see their fathers as rivals, and secretly want to kill them so they can take their place—a pattern he called the Oedipus Complex.

In healthy childhood development, the boy eventually begins to identify with the male, his father, and loses his desire to marry his mother. Failing to do this leads to a host of neurotic behavior. Freud believed that not identifying with the father was directly responsible for homosexuality in males. Freud also examined the development of young girls and felt he discovered a similar pattern he called the Electra Complex, named for another figure of Greek myth. These complexes represented repressed memories, unfulfilled desires and emotions which would go on to greatly influence adult behavior.

During this time, Freud suffered his own neurosis, battling depression, mood swings, and nightmares. He could never really enjoy his accomplishments and usually thought the books and articles he had written were terrible. He never clearly recognized his place in the world, or how respect for his work was growing.

Publishing Successes

First published in November of 1899, *The Interpretation of Dreams* was the first true psychoanalytic work. It explained how our lives are made up, not only of conscious choices, but also of unconscious desires.

While *Dreams* did not sell as many copies as Freud had hoped, Freud's hopes rarely matched reality. Still, the book's straightforward, non-technical style meant it was enjoyed by many who had never set foot in a medical school.

Soon after he completed *Dreams*, Freud began a new book. His previous book found meaning when we dream. *The Psychology of Everyday Life* would find meaning when we are awake.

Written in the same accessible style as *Dreams*, *The Psychology*'s exploration of day-to-day symbols helped make Freud a household name. Even today people who have never heard of the book know about "Freudian slips," which he described in a letter to Fliess: "You know how one can forget a name and substitute part of another one for it, you could swear it was correct, although invariably it turns out to be wrong."[3]

Pioneering Work

Freud's work would soon have as much influence on the twentieth century as Darwin had on the nineteenth. Prior to Darwin, most people believed animal species were unchanging throughout their time on earth. Darwin's theory of evolution proposed that all creatures "evolve," undergo changes, some quite profound.

Similarly, in Freud's time, most believed sexuality began at puberty. Children were viewed as innocent creatures, untouched by sexual thoughts or feelings. Freud believed that sexual impulses begin at birth.

Freud's theories of childhood sexuality were

even more controversial than Darwin's theory of evolution. Freud described the specific phases each child passes through. The oral phase occurs when a baby is breastfeeding; the anal phase is when a child undergoes toilet training; and finally the genital phase is when the child discovers his or her genitals as a source of pleasure. From age six until puberty, Freud believed children enter a latency period and sexual expression is dormant.

According to Freud people who do not successfully pass through a stage can become fixated. Unconscious conflicts between sexually driven fantasies and the repressive forces of shame, guilt, and morality created neuroses. Those who skip the latency period also developed neurosis.

With the publication of *Psychopathology*, "unconscious conflicts," and "Freudian slips" became popular topics for conversations across the world. Academics and others debated his theories. The book became a best-seller. While Freud was alive, it was published in a dozen different languages and almost as many new editions.

In addition to the "average reader," a growing number of doctors were intrigued by Freud's approach. One of them was Wilhelm Stekel, a local doctor who gave *Dreams* a positive review. In 1902, he approached Freud, suggesting they form a psychoanalysis discussion group. Freud agreed. He knew he needed to do more than just write books for his theories to gain acceptance. He also needed to train more analysts.

"The Wednesday Society"

In 1902, "The Wednesday Society" began. As the name suggests, it met every Wednesday, usually in Freud's home. Inside, a thick haze accumulated—many of the attendees smoked cigars in imitation of Freud. In a few years, the society attracted over two dozen regulars smoking and discussing psychoanalysis.

Some members, like Russian Max Eitingon were born to rich families, whereas others, like

Alfred Adler, grew up in poverty. Freud's fees were the equivalent of nearly $200 an hour today, and his practice focused on the upper classes. Adler was not opposed to high–fee-paying clients, but he worked mainly with the poor and working classes.

Meanwhile Freud worried that his most loyal advocates were Jewish. He knew this could be a problem. Anti-Semitism in Europe was on the rise yet again and some people would not listen to a Jewish doctor. Freud was therefore overjoyed when he received a letter from the Swiss (and Gentile) Carl Jung in April, 1906.

Jung

The son of a minister and an only child until age nine, Jung had been the focus of an increasingly disturbed mother. His father was often away. Before he was twenty, both of his parents had been institutionalized.

Jung's desire to understand his childhood and his parent's mental illness led him to psychiatry. For many mental health professionals, trying to understand their own problems is a driving factor long before they devote time to helping anyone else.

Jung was a successful professor and head of Zurich's Burgholzi Mental Hospital when he began studying Freud's writing. At Burgholzi, Jung organized a testing system which determined a patient's unconscious drives. This system relied on his understanding of Freud, although many of his colleagues dismissed the analyst's ideas.

When the two finally met at Freud's home in 1907, they spoke for thirteen hours. Jung did most of the talking and Freud quickly became a father figure for the man whose own father had been cruel and unavailable. Jung did all he could to champion Freud's ideas while traveling to Vienna as often as possible.

Group Conflicts

By 1909, the Wednesday Society was a diverse group of analysts, representing a variety of backgrounds. Although women were offered few opportunities outside of marriage or teaching, psychoanalysis was open to them and a number studied with Freud. During each meeting one member read his or her paper on an aspect of psychoanalysis. Afterward the group discussed

Sigmund Freud, Brill, Jones, Ferenczi, Hall, and Jung are photographed together here in 1909.

it. This could be brutal. Instead of focusing on the contents, they focused on the presenter. They discussed the writer's childhood experiences, repressions, drives, and sexual experiences while also analyzing the work.

Scientific discussions often become heated. In laboratories, researchers debate their work, disagreeing with each other on the journey toward discovery. However, the Wednesday Society did not just keep what worked and discard the rest. Instead, they were expected to be one hundred percent supportive of Freud's theories.

Musicologist Max Graf recalled, "the last and decisive word was always spoken by Freud himself, there was an atmosphere of the foundation of a religion in that room."[4]

Freud did not encourage independence—he was only interested in work supporting the research he had already done. Adler's independent thinking made a clash inevitable. Adler was driven by an insatiable curiosity, the same hunger for knowledge Freud had held as a young man.

Unlike many of the men in the group, Adler did not want a father figure. He considered Freud an inspiration for his work, but Adler did not mind arriving at opposing conclusions that displeased Freud.

Beginning with 1907's, "Study of Organ Inferiority and Its Psychological Compensation," Adler began working through ideas leading to his best known theory: the inferiority complex.

Adler believed all children suffer from feelings of inferiority because they are naturally smaller and weaker than adults. This creates an "inferiority complex" in adulthood. One of the ways children and adults struggle to overcome this is through what he called "aggressive drive."

"Fighting, wrestling, beating, biting and cruelties show the aggressive drive in its pure form. Its refinement and specialization lead to sports, competition, dueling, war, thirst for dominance and religious, social, national and race struggles."[5]

Adler also saw a need for affection as a basic drive. Children want to be hugged, complimented, and told they are loved. How well or how poorly their parents and other adults in their lives do this often determines how successful they are in forming loving relationships as adults.

While Freud accepted the way things were, and saw women's place as being traditional, Adler saw the times they lived in as responsible for many neuroses. To him "the arch evil of our culture, is the excessive preeminence of manliness."[6]

Visiting the States

In 1909, Freud and Jung were invited to give a series of lectures at Clark University in Worcester, Massachusetts. It would be Freud's first trip to the United States. Besides Jung he also took a Wednesday Society member, Sandor Ferenczi.

Freud did not travel well. The doctor was used to routine. His wife fixed the food he liked, set out his clothing, made sure he did not have to give a moment's thought to anything other than his work (and occasionally his family). Yet for someone who had devoted hours to psychoanalysis, Freud seemed unable to discern the reasons he had so much difficulty whenever his routine was upset.

Every Sunday he and his family traveled to his mother's house for a meal. Every Saturday night he would become violently ill. He never considered that anxiety might be behind his Saturday sickness. Instead he blamed whatever food Martha served him for the evening meal.

Before he even left Europe, Freud suffered a fainting spell, collapsing during a discussion between Jung and Ferenczi about preserved prehistoric corpses. When he recovered, Freud told Jung he was convinced Jung's unconscious desire to murder him was a repressed, Oedipus urge. Talking about burial rituals proved it. Jung was flabbergasted—he loved and admired Freud. If he had any Oedipal conflicts, Jung was certain he had dealt with them.

In the United States, Freud endured a nasty stomach illness which persisted for most of their time onshore. He blamed the country and the food he ate, but never the anxiety after his normal routine was disrupted by travel. In spite of the physical challenges, Freud's lectures were, to those who attended them, amazing. Speaking in German without notes and little preparation, he held the crowd's attention for hours with a discussion of his theories and their origin.

Despite the success of the American tour, trouble was on the horizon not only in Vienna but soon for the rest of the world as well.

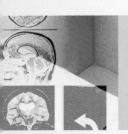

7

The War To
End All Wars

ALFRED ADLER DID NOT THINK HE WAS IN trouble. He was convinced his disagreements with Sigmund Freud would diminish once he explained himself. In 1911, Adler got his chance. Four meetings of the Wednesday Society were reserved for examining Adler's work. Whether he was forced to leave the group would ultimately be up to Freud.

When Adler presented his work he did not hold back. Adler felt the environment a child grew up in, and the greater society around him was at least as significant, if not more so, than sexual repression. He felt these issues created as many neuroses, and pointed out that, "The sexual references described by Freud are indeed found in neuroses. But my findings show that whatever one sees as sexual, behind it are much more important connections, namely the masculine protest disguised under sexuality. . . . I have seen my patients who have come to know their Oedipus complex very well, without feeling any improvement."[1]

Disagreements increased. Battle lines were drawn. There was little room for compromise as Wednesday members like Stekel and Graf sided with Adler. Most of the others opposed him, none as forcefully as Freud. He attacked Adler for minimizing how important sexual drives were. Freud was certain they were the motivating factor for all human behavior and neuroses.

Freud complimented Adler on how well written his book was, but felt it could permanently damage the psychoanalytic movement. Outsiders who read it would be confused by the lack of emphasis on sexuality. Disagreements within the Wednesday Society might make psychoanalysts seem like a group that could not make up their minds.

Eventually Adler resigned. Stekel, who had

begun the Wednesday group, also left to join Adler's organization, which became known as The Society for Free Psychoanalytic Research.

Further Disagreements

The conflicts were not over. Jung agreed with some of Adler's points. By 1912, only Freud was more prominent—Jung was President of the International Psychoanalytic Society and editor for *Jahrbruch*, a major psychoanalytic journal. He endured his peer's jealousy while developing his own unique theories.

Freud viewed Jung as a son; and the younger man greatly admired the doctor. The growing breach between them was far more traumatic for Freud than the one with Adler. Adler and Jung treated illnesses Freud never came into contact with. Many of Jung's patients were schizophrenic, a frightening disorder marked by hallucinations, fits of rage and violence, and the inability to connect with the outside world. Even today the disease is barely understood and usually treated with powerful medications. In Jung's time, there were no such medical approaches. Therapy for schizophrenics varied widely and often the treatments were nearly as painful as the disorder.

Jung genuinely felt for most other people while Freud only liked patients who were bright and interesting. Once Jung introduced Freud to a patient he had been treating. Afterward, discussing her case, Freud casually asked how he could spend so much time treating such an ugly woman.

Freud's last experience treating schizophrenics came during his psychiatric rotation thirty years before. That did not stop him advising Jung about the importance of repressed sexual drives in schizophrenia.

Jung disagreed with the analysis, noting in a letter that, "The loss of reality function in schizophrenia cannot be reduced to repression of libido defined as sexual hunger. Not by me, at any rate."[2]

Jung examined his successes and failures working with schizophrenics in the book *Symbols of Transformation*. The work also explored areas of disagreement with Freud and examined the roles of eastern religion and mythology. The book was worse for Freud than a simple disagreement. His own book, *Totem and Taboo*, also explored the role of mythology. By then, the two differed not just in their approaches to psychoanalysis, but also in their approach to research. While Jung's mind was open to all the possibilities, Freud confided to Ferenczi, "I'm reading fat books without real interest, since I know the conclusions already."[3]

Disagreements between Freud and Jung grew hostile. The two tried to repair their rift at a meeting in Munich, but that accomplished little. Worse, Freud suffered another fainting spell.

Freud finally wrote a letter, saying, "I propose that we abandon our personal relations entirely. I shall lose nothing by it, for my only emotional tie with you has long been a thin thread—the lingering effect of past disappointments."

"I accede to your wish that we abandon our personal relations," Jung wrote back. "The rest is silence."[4]

Jung went on to develop a branch of

Carl Gustav Jung (above) broke away from Freud both professionally and personally in 1912.

psychoanalysis very different from Freud's. Examining the collective unconscious, his later works would look at this theory that certain belief systems and mythologies are common to all people and linked our stories and ideas. His views on creativity inspired writers, artists, and later filmmakers.

Unrest in Europe

While Freud and his Wednesday Society were arguing, larger disagreements were boiling over across Europe. Arguments over borders grew along with nationalism—the feeling that one's country was superior to others. On December 9, 1912, commenting on the world situation, Freud told his friend Oskar Pfister, "The expectation of war almost takes our breath away."[5]

Less than two years later, many others felt their breath taken away after a Bosnian militant assassinated Austro-Hungary's Archduke Franz Ferdinand in Sarajevo, Serbia. Weeks after that single act, the leaders of Austria-Hungary and Serbia continued to trade angry words. Finally, in late July, 1914, Austria-Hungary declared war. Freud's immediate response was one of intense patriotism. "Perhaps for the first time in thirty years, I feel myself an Austrian and would like just once more to give this rather unpromising empire a chance."[6]

Freud's sudden patriotism was matched by many across Europe. Germany joined Austria-Hungary as an ally, while Britain and France (who had hoped to remain neutral) opposed them. The United States would later enter the conflict as well.

Many historians consider World War I the first truly modern war—and modern warfare extracted enormous casualties on its participants. Against the fearsome barrage of relatively new devices like tanks, machine guns, and chemical weapons, soldiers either huddled in trenches or ran straight toward the enemy. Thousands of men were mowed down in these battles, thousands more died from diseases that ran rampant in the wet, dirty trenches.

The Toll of War

From the first month of the war, mental health issues surfaced. Soldiers froze in battle or ran away from combat. Survivors battled nightmares, odd muscle twitches and paralysis. The doctors called it "shell shock," under the mistaken impression it was related to the soldier's proximity to loud explosions.

Ernst Simmel was a German physician assigned to a hospital near the front lines. As he encountered soldiers suffering from "shell shock," he noticed similarities to the symptoms displayed by hysterics. He was familiar with the work Freud did thirty years before, and concluded a traumatic event (or series of events) caused the soldiers condition. That trauma was often buried in their unconscious. He began treating the shell-shocked soldiers using the cathartic method and hypnosis.

His work came to Freud's attention when his friend Karl Abraham wrote to him, complaining that Simmel "has not yet in any way moved beyond the Breuer-Freud point of view, . . . sexuality does not play an essential part either in war neuroses or in analytic treatment."[7]

Freud believed shell-shocked soldiers were suffering from the effects of childhood trauma and the war only brought their problems to the surface. He also felt their issues would disappear when they returned to civilian life.

Sadly, this was incorrect. Besides the nearly ten million soldiers who died, over 250,000 were declared mentally disabled, their minds permanently altered by wartime traumas. Thousands more carried the psychic pain of combat with them for the rest of their lives.

His narrow view of shell-shocked soldiers was the same as it was of his patients. As biographer Frank J. Sulloway notes, "Time and time again, Freud saw in his patients what psychoanalytic theory led him to look for and then to interpret the way he did."[8]

Along with Freud's three sons and several male patients, most of his female patients had fathers or husbands connected to the war effort.

With fewer patients, Freud relied on writing to pay the bills. Suffering under stringent rationing, he occasionally asked to be paid in cigars and food.

Loss and Grief

Life did not improve after the war. The Treaty of Versailles in 1918 altered borders while Germany, Austria, and their allies were expected to pay back the cost of the war. Their citizens suffered terrible shortages of food and heating oil. Besides starving and freezing, a flu epidemic swept through, taking the life of Freud's daughter Sophie in 1920, along with twenty-million more worldwide.

In the midst of so much sadness and loss, Freud continued to write. In 1920, his book *Beyond the Pleasure Principle* was published. It was another of his widely read books. Beyond that work's success was the publication of a theory he began formulating during the war. In addition to a drive for sex, Freud saw another drive as the death drive—Thanatos—the drive which motivates countries to war and individuals to fight and die.

Some wondered if personal losses affected his work but Freud denied it, claiming Sophie had died after he had finished writing down the theories.

Anna Freud

Saddled with the loss of one daughter, Freud focused on another. Anna grew up in Sophie's shadow, convinced

A photograph of Freud's daughter Sophie, taken in 1898.

she was the "ugly one." A photo from when the girls were six and four shows two remarkably similar children, both with dark hair and pretty faces, but Sophie is smiling, playing to the camera while Anna looks at the ground. Anna grew up looking down.

During the Wednesday Society meetings she would listen from upstairs as they debated psychoanalysis. Freud discouraged his children from becoming analysts, but Anna would not be deterred. Shy and quiet about most things, she pursued a career in analysis with a singular focus. She spent years being analyzed by her father (he even used her recollections in his writing, changing her identity) and became a successful analyst of children.

She also fell in love with Ernest Jones, Freud's colleague and future biographer. Freud refused to give his blessing and convinced Jones not to pursue the relationship. He also wrote Anna, saying "I have not thought of giving you the freedom of choice your sisters enjoyed," so while her older siblings married, Freud pointed out that, "I would like to believe that you would find it more difficult to make such a decision for life without [my] consent."[9]

A few years later, she became interested in another colleague of her father's, Hans Lamperl, but again Freud discouraged her.

Anna never married. She spent the rest of her life attending her father's needs, giving lectures, and analyzing. Her books on psychoanalysis are widely respected, and she also has offered biographers a view of Freud they might have otherwise not received.

Soon Freud needed all the help he could get. In 1923, he discovered a lump in his mouth, and went to a doctor. It was cancerous, the result of his decades-long twenty-cigar-a-day habit. That

Freud's daughter Anna in a photograph taken in 1914.

same year, Freud's grandson, Heinerle, died. "I don't think I have ever experienced such grief. . . . Fundamentally everything has lost its meaning for me," Freud later wrote.[10]

Continuing Work

Yet in the midst of so much loss, Freud was tremendously productive. In 1921 he had published *Group Psychology and the Analysis of the Ego* followed by 1923's, *The Ego and the Id.* Dealing with a new model for the mind, it radically changed the conscious, pre-conscious, and unconscious divisions from *The Interpretation of Dreams.* Instead, he described the constant battles between the ego, the id, and the super-ego. The ego he viewed as our conscious selves—the way we see ourselves, the person we have become. The id are repressed drives, the

Anna Freud at age forty-five in 1940.

things we want to do but usually do not. The super-ego is our conscience, our belief in what is right and what is wrong.

Although Freud published other books in the 1920s, these two stood out. Over the next several years, he also examined anxiety in 1926's *Inhibitions, Symptoms and Anxiety* and religion in 1927's *The Future of an Illusion*.

Even as Freud's influence was growing among members of the psychiatric community, another man's power was on the rise. Adolph Hitler was a failed painter whose calls for national pride met with an enthusiastic audience in Germany. Focusing his rage and the rage of his followers upon Jews, Hitler blamed them for the economic problems going on in that country.

In 1930, his National Socialist (Nazi) Party was elected to 111 seats in the Reichstag, the German congress. They were the second largest power and they used their influence. In 1933, they convinced the president Paul von Hindenburg to appoint Hitler chancellor following the burning of the Reichstag. After elections put the Nazi party in the majority, Hitler assumed dictatorial powers abolishing freedom of the press and freedom of speech.

In Vienna, Hitler's rise worried many in the Jewish community. However, they had suffered through anti-Semitism before, and most did not believe his actions in Germany would affect them.

They were wrong.

Nazi Propaganda

In May of 1933, the Nazi's attack on Jews became personal for Sigmund Freud. The Propaganda Minister considered Freud dangerous. In Berlin, the books of many Jewish people and others were publicly burned. A declaration was posted near the inferno: "Against the soul-destroying glorification of the instinctual life, for the nobility of the human soul! I consign to the flames the writings of the school of Sigmund Freud."[11]

Despite the risks, Freud refused to leave Vienna. Partly it was the same stubborn strength he had shown his whole life, and partly it was illness. Some of his jaw had been removed in surgeries, and he was fitted with an uncomfortable prosthesis he called "The Monster." Needing to be taken care of, the last thing he wanted to do was embark on a difficult trip. Other Jews left Vienna as quickly as they could, including many

A photograph of Sigmund Freud taken in 1931, near the end of his life.

members of the Wednesday Society and other psychoanalytic organizations. Freud waited until it was almost too late.

In 1938, the Austrian chancellor was forced to resign, and the Nazis were allowed to invade the country. It was a horrific time. Jewish people were beaten in the streets by angry mobs as police looked on.

Last Days in London

With powerful friends, and considerable bribes to government officials, Freud and his wife left Austria, settling at 20 Maresfield Gardens in London. Not everyone in his family escaped. Nazis put his sisters in concentration camps. In 1942, Freud's sister Adolphine would die at Theresienstadt transit camp, while Mitzi, Rosa, and Paula would lose their lives at the Treblinka extermination camp.

Despite his illness, he continued seeing patients and finished the controversial *Moses and Monotheism* along with *An Outline of Psychoanalysis*.

Freud warned his friends to visit as soon as

they could—he knew his days were limited. Suffering tremendously, he convinced his doctor and Anna to give him an overdose of morphine. He died on September 23, 1939.

His theories lived on, and by the 1950s a majority of psychiatrists relied on at least some of his work. However, by the 1960s, drug therapies were replacing analysis and Freud's ideas were falling out of favor.

Freud's Legacy

Freud saw himself first and foremost as a scientist. Throughout his life, he believed that psychoanalytic concepts could eventually be described in terms of clinical and physical processes. After his death, many wondered if psychoanalysis was a science.

Fellow Viennese, Karl Popper, developed a philosophy of examining scientific theories that looked at whether or not a theory was testable, or what he called falsifiable. That is, in the law of conservation of matter we would expect that a piece of paper set on fire would become other

A photo and bust on display at the Freud Museum in London.

things but not disappear. It could become ash, or smoke—and indeed it does. If an experiment was constructed to disprove this, if paper could be made to disappear entirely, then the law would be falsifiable.

One of the criticisms of Freud's theories is that by their nature they explain all behavior in a way that cannot be tested or disproved. Because of this, many consider Freud's theories unscientific. However, recent studies have begun to bring the ideas of Freud renewed popularity. Repression, dream states, the unconscious have been demonstrated in studies and many scientists who study the brain are looking to Freud's theories because, as Nobel laureate Eric R. Kandel points out, "it is still the most coherent and intellectually satisfying view of the mind."[12]

Activities

▶ **Activity One: DREAM JOURNAL**

For this activity, you will need one notebook, one pen, or a pen light, one flashlight—preferably with a yellow or red filter.

Everyone dreams. Asleep, when we reach a state called Rapid Eye Movement (REM), our mind forms images, images that Sigmund Freud analyzed for their symbols. The most important part to analyzing dreams is remembering them. This is a skill.

Our most vivid dream recollections occur right after we wake up. The rest of the day can crowd out our memories, or change them. Eventually they go back to the unconscious. Instead, upon waking turn on the flashlight. Keeping your room dim can help you stay in between the conscious and unconscious state.

If you have a pen that lights up, you can

eliminate the flashlight. The idea is to write everything you recall from the dream, without pause. Do not analyze it or think about it, just record it. Do this every day for a week or so. Do you discover patterns? Are you running in several dreams, or is a certain person regularly represented?

Finding the meaning of dreams can be difficult and subjective. There are a variety of books that look at dreams, beginning with Freud's. The most important thing is to write them down.

▶ **Activity Two: MAKE YOUR OWN RORSCHACH TEST**

For this activity, you will need several friends, a notebook, finger paints, and blank paper.

Just as dreams are subject to interpretation, so too, is another technique used to determine one's unconscious. Developed by Hermann Rorschach, the "ink blot" test is called a "psychological projective of personality" because the subject projects their personality onto what they see. Usually consisting of ten ink blots, the test is still used today. Because of this, actual Rorschach tests are kept secret. But you can make your own.

First, pour a small amount of finger paint onto the paper. Fold it in the middle, then unfold. Now you have your own inkblot.

What does it look like? Pass the blot among a small group. Have each person write what they think it is on a page of the notebook, turn to a blank page and pass it to the next person. After everyone is done, look at the results. Does everyone see similar things? Different things? Just as one can interpret dreams, interpreting what a person sees in an inkblot can be very subjective. But it can also be fun.

Chronology

1856—Born on May 6 in Freiberg, Moravia.

1859—Family moves from Freiberg to Leipzig.

1860—Family settles in Vienna.

1865—Enters Leopoldstadter Gymnasium school.

1873—Enrolls at the University of Vienna where he will study zoology and philosophy before focusing on medicine.

1881—Graduates as doctor of medicine.

1882—Engaged to Martha Bernays.

1882–1885—Works in Vienna General Hospital.

1885–1886—Studies in Paris under Jean Martin Charcot where he learns about hypnosis and its applications for treating hysteria.

1886—Leaves hospital and open his private practice. Marries Martha Bernays twice; first in a civil ceremony, then in a religious one two days later.

1887—Begins treating hysterics at his practice relying on a combination of hypnosis and electroshock.

1893–1895—Begins collaborating with Josef Breuer for the book *Studies on Hysteria*.

1895—Writes a rough draft of *Project for a Scientific*

Psychology, which is an attempt to work out psychological theories based on neurological terms. Work is later abandoned.

1895—Anna Freud is born on December 3.

1896—First use of the term "psychoanalysis"; death of his father.

1897—Begins self-analysis; recognizes the importance of infantile sexuality and develops his theory of the Oedipus complex.

1899—Publishes *The Interpretation of Dreams.*

1901—*The Psychopathology of Everyday Life* is published; introduction of the "Freudian slip."

1902—Founding of the Wednesday Psychological Society.

1906—Freud meets Swiss psychiatrist Carl Gustav Jung.

1909—Freud and Jung give the first lectures on psychoanalysis in America.

1912—Jung returns to U.S.

1913—*Totem and Taboo* is published.

1914—Secession of Jung from the official psychoanalytic movement.

1919—Observes soldiers traumatized by the war.

1920—Death of daughter, Sophie. Publishes *Beyond the Pleasure Principle,* which introduces the new theories of the "death drive."

1921—*Group Psychology and the Analysis of the Ego* is published.

1923—*The Ego and the Id* is published. The book deals with a new account of the structure of the mind, revising the "conscious/pre-conscious/unconscious" distinction found in *The Interpretation of Dreams*.

1923—Diagnosed with cancer.

1926—*Inhibitions, Symptoms and Anxiety* is published. Freud makes anxiety the cornerstone of his developmental theory.

1927—*The Future of an Illusion* is published. The book is a consideration of the origins and function of religion. It is here that Freud explicitly states his atheism.

1930—*Civilization and its Discontents* is published. The book is a profoundly pessimistic account of the irreconcilability of personal drives and the demands of society.

1933—Freud's books, along with other psychoanalytic works, are publicly burned by the Nazis in Berlin.

1938—Moves to London NW3.

1939—Dies in London on September 23.

Chapter Notes

Chapter 1. Dreaming

1. Sigmund Freud, *The Interpretation of Dreams* (Oxford: Oxford University Press 1999), pp. 84–94.

2. Ibid.

3. Ralph Waldo Emerson, *Historic Notes of Life and Letters in New England* <http://www.vcu.edu/engweb/transcendentalism/authors/emerson/essays/historicnotes.html> (October 4, 2005).

4. Peter Medawar, "Victims of Psychiatry," Review of *The Victim is Always the Same*, by I. S. Cooper, *The New York Review of Books*, January 23, 1975, p. 17.

Chapter 2. Turmoil

1. Sigmund Freud, *The Interpretation of Dreams* (Oxford: Oxford University Press 1999), p. 151.

2. Sigmund Freud, "Feminity," *The New Introductory Lectures on Psycho-Analysis*, vol. 22 (Standard Edition, 1933), pp.121–123.

3. *The Complete Letters of Sigmund Freud to Wilhelm Fliess: 1887–1904*, Jeffrey M. Masson, ed. and trans. (Cambridge, Mass: Harvard University Press, 1985), p. 268.

4. *Sigmund Freud, His Life in Pictures and Words*, Ernst Lucie Freud and Ilse Grubrich-Simitis, eds., trans. Christine Trollope (New York: Harcourt, Brace, Jovanovich, 1976), p. 134.

5. Ernest Jones, *The Life and Works of Sigmund Freud*, Vol. 1 (New York: Basic Books, 1957), p. 142.

6. Sigmund Freud, *Autobiographical Study*, Postscript p. 8.

Chapter 3. **Choices**

1. John P. Riddell, "The Last Illness and Death of President, General, and Masonic Brother George Washington," *George Washington Masonic National Memorial*, n.d., <http//www.gwmemorial.org/History/gw_history/History020.htm> (April 29, 2005).

2. Sigmund Freud, *Autobiographical Study*, Postscript 72.

3. Ernest Jones, *The Life and Works of Sigmund Freud*, Vol. 1 (New York: Basic Books, 1957), p. 44.

4. *The Complete Letters of Sigmund Freud to Wilhelm Fliess: 1887–1904*, Jeffrey M. Masson, ed. and trans. (Cambridge, Mass: Harvard University Press, 1985), p. 374; and *Freud As We Knew Him*, Ruitenbeek, Hendrik M., ed. (Detroit: Wayne State University Press, 1973), p. 145.

5. Theodor Reik, *Listening With the Third Ear: The Inner Experience of a Psychoanalyst* (New York: Farrar, Strauss, 1948), p. 7.

6. Ernest Jones, *The Life and Works*, Vol. 1, p. 111.

7. Peter Gay, *Freud: A Life for Our Times* (New York: W. W. Norton & Co, 1998), p. 39.

8. Sigmund Freud, *An Autobiographical Study*, p. 10.

9. Edward Shorter, *A History of Psychiatry* (New York: John Wiley and Sons, 1997), pp. 76–77.

10. Sigmund Freud, *On the History of the Psychoanalytic Movement*, vol. 15 (New York: Penguin, 1914), p. 71.

11. Shorter, 1997, pp. 76–77.

12. Ernest Jones, *The Life and Works*, Vol. 1, p. 84.

13. Ibid.

14. Freud, *On the History of the Psychoanalytic Movement*, p. 71.

Chapter 4. Chimney Sweeping

1. Sigmund Freud, *An Autobiographical Study*, pp. 15–16.

2. Peter Gay, *Freud: A Life for Our Times* (New York: W. W. Norton & Co, 1998), p. 53.

3. Ronald W. Clark, *Freud: The Man and the Cause* (New York: Random House, 1980), p. 54.

4. Gay, p. 64.

5. Sigmund Freud, *Five Lectures*, p. 22.

6. Ibid, p. 9.

7. Gay, p. 71.

8. Sigmund Freud, *Studies in Hysteria*, pp. 88, 103.

9. Sigmund Freud, *Sexuality in the Aetiology of the Neurosis*, pp. 263, 269.

10. Gay, p. 67.

11. Sigmund Freud, *Studies in Hysteria*, p. 4.

12. *The Complete Letters of Sigmund Freud to Wilhelm Fliess: 1887–1904*, Jeffrey M. Masson, ed. and trans. (Cambridge, Mass: Harvard University Press, 1985), pp.160–161.

Chapter 5. The Dream

1. *The Complete Letters of Sigmund Freud to Wilhelm Fliess: 1887–1904*, Jeffrey M. Masson, ed. and trans. (Cambridge, Mass: Harvard University Press, 1985), p. 16.

2. Peter Gay, *Freud: A Life for Our Times* (New York: W. W. Norton & Co, 1998), p. 78.

3. *Complete Letters*, p. 158.

4. Sigmund Freud, *The Interpretation of Dreams* (Oxford: Oxford University Press, 1999), pp. 84–94.

Chapter 6. Complexes

1. *The Complete Letters of Sigmund Freud to Wilhelm Fliess: 1887–1904*, Jeffrey M. Masson, ed. and trans. (Cambridge, Mass: Harvard University Press, 1985), p. 193.

2. Ibid., p. 314.

3. Ibid., p. 324.

4. Louis Breger, *Freud: Darkness in the Midst of Vision* (New York: John Wiley & Sons, 2000), p. 174.

5. Ibid., p. 199.

6. Ibid., p. 200.

Chapter 7. The War To End All Wars

1. Louis Breger, *Freud: Darkness in the Midst of Vision* (New York: John Wiley & Sons, 2000), p. 201.

2. *The Freud-Jung Letters: The Correspondence Between Sigmund Freud & C. G. Jung*, W. McGuire, ed. (Princeton, N.J.: Princeton University Press, 1974), p. 471.

3. Breger, p. 227.

4. *The Freud-Jung Letters*, p. 540.

5. Peter Gay, *Freud: A Life for Our Times* (New York: W. W. Norton & Co, 1998), p. 345.

6. Ernest Jones, *The Life and Works of Sigmund Freud*, Vol. 2 (New York: Basic Books, 1957), p. 169.

7. Breger, p. 258.

8. Frank J. Sulloway, *Freud: Biologist of the Mind* (New York: Basic Books 1979), p. 498.

9. Breger, p. 304.

10. Sigmund Freud, *Letters of Sigmund Freud*, Ernst L. Freud, ed., Tania and James Stern, trans. (New York: Dover, 1960), pp. 343–344.

11. "Burning Books," *Freud Museum London*, n.d., <http://www.freud.org.uk/bookburning.html> (June 2, 2005).

12. Mark Solms, "Freud Returns" *Scientific American*, May 2004, Vol. 290, Issue 5, p. 82.

Glossary

analyst—Individual who has studied analysis and is able to analyze patients.

anti-Semitism—Prejudice towards people of Jewish background.

catharsis—The effect of cleansing or emptying oneself emotionally or psychologically.

collaboration—The cooperative effort between two or more people toward a common goal.

control—In scientific research a standard of comparison for checking experiments.

defense mechanism—The unconscious technique used to protect a person from shame, anxiety, or loss of self esteem.

denial—Refusing to acknowledge an often painful truth.

ego—Largely conscious part of the mind.

Electra Complex—The theory that girls at age five are in love with their fathers and want to get rid of their mothers.

free association—Thinking of whatever comes to mind without holding back.

Gentile—Someone, especially a Christian, who is not Jewish.

hysteria—Condition marked by physical symptoms such as paralysis and tingling without any obvious physical cause. Considered to be a "woman's disease" in the 19th century.

iconoclast—Individual who fights against traditional society.

id—The unconscious drives of our mind.

Inferiority Complex—Lack of self esteem and belief in oneself.

neurosis—Mental or emotional disorder without a physical cause.

Oedipus Complex—Freud's theory of how boys at age five wish to marry their mothers and kill their fathers.

pleasure principle—The drive for life and pleasure (Eros).

psychoanalysis—Freud's methods and theories of the unconscious mind and ways to treat its problems.

repression—The way the consciousness blocks out memories that are too painful to deal with.

seduction theory—Belief that all neurotic behavior is the result of childhood sexual abuse.

sublimation—Channeling the energy from unacceptable behavior into socially acceptable activities such as writing, music or art.

super ego—The conscience of the mind.

transference—Act of treating a therapist like an important person from patient's past, such as a parent.

trauma—An emotional shock which creates lasting psychological damage and often results in a neuroses.

unconscious—Part of the mind immune to conscious resistance or control.

Further Reading

Books

Bloom, Harold, ed. *Sigmund Freud.* Broomall, Pa.: Chelsea House, 1985.

Gogerly, Liz. *Sigmund Freud.* Austin, Tex.: Raintree Publishers, 2003.

Muckenhoupt, Margaret. *Sigmund Freud: Explorer of the Unconscious.* New York: Oxford University Press, 1997.

Reef, Catherine. *Sigmund Freud: Pioneer of the Mind.* Clarion Books, 2001.

Internet Addresses

Freud Museum in London
http://www.freud.org.uk/

Sigmund Freud—Life and Work
http://www.freudfile.org/

Time 100: Sigmund Freud
http://www.time.com/time/time100/scientist/profile/freud.html

Index